PROPHECY MECHANIC

PROPHECY
MECHANIC

poems

Chad Sokolovsky

QUERCUS REVIEW PRESS
MODESTO, CA
2017

QUERCUS REVIEW PRESS POETRY SERIES
Sam Pierstorff, *Editor*

Published by Quercus Review Press
Department of English
Modesto Junior College
quercusreviewpress.com

Cover Art Image by Mitchell Sokolovsky
Cover Art Photograph by Rebecca Wang
Author Photograph by Philip Johnson

Interior Design by Hakeem Pierstorff,
Artistic Director, Quercus Review Press

Printed on acid-free paper
10 9 8 7 6 5 4 3 2 1

Requests for permissions to make copies of any part of this work should be mailed to: Permissions, Quercus Review Press, Modesto Jr. College, 435 College Avenue, Modesto, CA 95350

ISBN-13: 978-0692925393
ISBN-10: 0692925392

Publications by Quercus Review Press (QRP) are made possible with the support of the English Department at Modesto Junior College. A portion of the proceeds from the sale of this book will benefit creative writing scholarships at Modesto Junior College.

— For Lucy, Mitchell, and Sebastian

"One can have, it turns out, an affection for the war years."
— Steve Martin

CONTENTS

1. SUPERHEROES DON'T EAT CAROB CHIPS

2. AFFECTION FOR THE WAR YEARS

3. POST-GRAMMATICAL STRESS DISORDER

4. EAVESDROPPING ON ANGRY WEATHER

5. SMOOTH CURSIVE & RAW OYSTERS

1.

SUPERHEROES DON'T EAT CAROB CHIPS

"I came into the world very young,
in an age that was very old."
— Erik Satie

MEMORIAL DAY

We used to burn ants with a magnifying glass
watching their thoraxes smolder on the sidewalk

Honed the bayonets of our sharp tongues
against orders to divide fractions and decode Dickens

Legos always made for shitty swords but we kept interlocking
mismatched bricks together like ill-equipped field medics

Any L-shaped scrap of wood was a gun
but a pointed finger and a flintlock thumb would do in a pinch

Armed with a #2 pencil to battle a Scantron
with its green ovals like landing lights in a storm

Girls were mushroom clouds blooming towards
the shallow trenches of our sunken chests

Drowned out by the screaming of air raid sirens
as the bomb doors of their new bodies slowly opened overhead.

4 LETTER WORDS

I learned to be a statue in Mr. Johns' fifth grade class
when I was caught floating a folded note across
to Jenny, who buried me with her kamikaze eyes

that I plummeted into during social studies. I was
sentenced to fifteen minutes of standing motionless
next to my desk beneath scale models of B-17 bombers

suspended from the acoustical-tiled ceiling like an artillery
gray sky. I could imagine Mr. Johns carefully applying the insignia
decals to the plastic wings in the foxhole of his empty apartment

and plotting bombing runs through our class when we
were caught smuggling an arsenal of profanity under
our tongues like the little shits we were.

WHAT I LEARNED FROM
SATURDAY MORNING CARTOONS

The Flash reminded all the fat kids
that they'd never run fast enough
to qualify for the President's Physical
Fitness award, or do enough chin-ups
to draw girls to the flames beating
beneath their Tough Skin corduroys.
We would never be able to sprout gills
and breathe underwater, read the dry dreams
of horny blue-finned tuna
or telepathically teach a school
of butterfly fish the calculus
of moon trajectories they only see
through the deflected ripples of passing waves.

We dribbled puberty down our chins
over bowls of Captain Crunch
while Wonder Woman taught us
that S&M with a truth-telling
golden lasso was just good clean fun.
And while Superman could straighten
twisted steel pylons in his sleep,
he would never know the struggle
of hand-me downs, the cruel architecture
of braces, or the trepidation of crowded
freshman hallways being stuffed
in a death-stench filled locker
of moist gym socks: the stuff
that teaches you to suck it up.

My arch nemesis was Jimmy
the paperboy who slugged my stomach
on a regular basis with a tightly gripped
fist of *fuck you.*

Armed with my only secret powers
of *stop, drop, and roll* I would climb
into the top bunk each night,
cover my ears and hide like a stow away
trying to silence my heart
pounding like adolescence
at the door begging to come in.

MATERNAL INSTINCTS

The sidewalk shatters
like plate glass under
the first drops of a storm
while you thought about
our first house
that always leaked in the rain,
when my brother and I
would safety-pin towels
around our necks
and fly over our neighborhood
in one ambivalent leap
over domestic disturbances,
empty cupboards,
and blank checkbooks.
But somehow you managed
to lasso our ankles
and rein us in before
our dishtowel capes
faded into the soupy
Pacifica fog,
sometime long before
the little white pills
stared at you
from the nightstand;
the night dad came
home just in time.

PEZ

I want to bend
your superhero head
back and extract
the chalky candy brick
from your neck,
then raise your
spring-loaded spine
to ready the next piece
for when I'll bite into
your hard sugar spleen
and crack your
cherry kidneys
between my teeth
because I can't
imagine what your
insides must taste like
or what it would
be like to massage
them between
the hungry ridges
of my fingertips
that sweat like saliva
glands every time I think
about devouring them.
As if I were performing
a candy appendectomy
by removing all the
unnecessary organs
evolution no longer
had any use for.

PULLING WEEDS

I would ride my black Huffy BMX
past the dumpster bins huddled
against the back of the Pizza Hut
like 5 o'clock shadows on concrete.

Pacifica, 1983, I was 10, we lived
two blocks from the ocean
and she slept across the street
on pillows of dreams
I only wanted to run around in.

My first love, she was 11
and never really knew how her soft
brown curls glided through
the playground of my mind.

July, I went to pull weeds
and dead grass from her back patio
because her mom promised
a rainbow sherbert from
the Thrifty Drugstore as payment.

And as pathetic as it sounds
to do yard work just to observe
the way her slivers of fingers
carved spirals in the soil,

let's face it, I would have done
anything to have an excuse
to just be near her when she plucked
the cap off Dr. Pepper chap stick
that made me drool.

Perhaps you could say it was illegal child labor
to blister my virgin palms amputating

dandelion wishes from grass
because I wasn't even old enough

to know how to touch myself yet
or what certain parts could do
or why I would count the number
of concentric circles on her fingerprints
because I notice details—

    my inverted reflection dancing in her irises
    the miniature goose bumps peaking past cotton sleeves
    the way the right heel of her Mary Jane's slanted left
    because she always stepped slightly sideways
    to avoid puddles and cracks.

I did not yet comprehend fibers of nerve endings
telegraphing up my spine charging brain fragment filaments
like a 100 watt bulb in my brain when she held my hand.

Sequential sparks peaking a science I didn't speak.
I didn't know what love meant.
I didn't know why I would massacre nature
just to be near her, or why my mother chose
that day to teach me a lesson:

        Countless warnings not to leave my bike
        unattended but I did it anyway.
        Hours passed and I couldn't find the bike
        my mother hid in the garage.

I sobbed into my blistered hands
and swallowed hard to tell my mom
it was stolen. But she just grinned and said, "I know."

But she didn't.
It was love mom, and you didn't understand
why I'd abandon my orphan bike on the steps

and run across the street to partake
in the frivolous task of pulling weeds,
as if I could stop photosynthesis,
chemistry, or my own tiny heart
pounding out rhythms I still struggle to hear.

SAN MATEO BRIDGE

We filed out
half-asleep onto the shoulder.
My rain-drenched pajamas
and a 2-foot high concrete
guard could barely hold
back my 7-year-old urge
to step over.

The night was as suffocating
as being smothered in grandma's
cardigan and that dreaded goodbye kiss
drenched in witch hazel.
As I choked on the rain
clogging my nose,
her 99-cent perfume
never smelled so sweet.

The deluge was as unrelenting
as a blacksmith obsessed with perfection.
The wind cut like a newly honed blade,
sharpened by the racket of colliding vehicles,
as our Datsun lay helpless against the onslaught.

We huddled together
until someone rescued
us from that narrow curb.
They said it was the distributor cap,
but all I cared about
were my abandoned shoes
still sleeping in the backseat.

HEALTH FOOD

My brother and I would have done anything
to get away from mom's cooking, because
when we were little, she went through that
herbal, health food, vitamin-saturated phase
in which my brother and I were subjected
to all kinds of cruel experiments involving
blue-green algae, spirulina, and fiber supplements
because we weren't "regular" enough. But how
often do you need to shit when you're
only eight years old anyway?

And this nasty thick concoction that tasted
like it was made from tree bark and alfalfa sprouts
called *Black Drought* that we never knew
was a laxative mom made us guzzle by the cup
making elementary school toilets
our worst enemy. We hated every minute
of it as if we detested the very idea
of being healthy because all we ever really wanted
were greasy french fries and anything
that came inside a Happy Meal.

And while the other kids opened their lunches
with this look of Christmas morning wonder,
my brother and I always knew that something with
zero fat, zero cholesterol, and zero flavor
awaited us as we unsnapped the hinges
on our Dukes of Hazzard lunch boxes.

I didn't know why we lived on food stamps
and plain yellow boxes of food that just said
Rice and *Cereal* because we were pale white,
stick skinny and plenty nerdy enough without
having to nibble on rice cakes in the cafeteria
like starving rabbits. And how were girls

ever going to like me when all I had to trade
at lunch were fake candy bars
made from carob chips?

It didn't matter how cool you were
because it was really sugar and grease
that determined the hierarchy in the lunchroom
and we were at the bottom of the pecking order,
not like that little shit Jonathan whose mother
would hand deliver McDonald's to him
every day while the other kids flocked around
like fucking seagulls just waiting for one stray
french fry to fall their way, like holy pilgrims
around an altar as if an apparition of the Virgin Mary
herself appeared in a grease stain
on the side of that McDonald's bag
right in between Grimace and the Hamburglar.

But not my brother and I, because if someone
out there made broccoli-cauliflower swirl flavored
ice cream, shit you could bet it was in our freezer.

Deep down I always knew mom meant well,
but that never stopped us from trying to smuggle
home pixie sticks like cocaine in the folds
of our jackets, and shoplifting M&M's
from the bulk bins in Safeway, and it's no wonder
that she never gave us any sugar, because
when we finally got it, we acted all twitchy,
nervous and irritating, and we couldn't ever shut up

as if sugar was our drug and we were strung out
like crack addicts, always plotting and scheming
where we were going to get our next fix,
trying to figure out which action figures
we were going to have to trade away
on the playground just to get a sample
of what a real Snicker's bar tasted like.

2.

AFFECTION
FOR THE
WAR YEARS

"There is no terror in the bang,
only in the anticipation of it."
— Alfred Hitchcock

QUESTIONS

What if my grandmother didn't stop that one night
and fall for the charms of a Russian bartender mixing a scotch and soda?
Would I be French or Guatemalan?

Or maybe I would have ended up as a scientist studying
the metabolism of ruby-throated hummingbirds,
the tornado factory of their tiny hearts conscripting wings
to carve figure eights into the bright canvas of the afternoon.

These are the "What would happen if..." types of questions
to chew on when fan blades are slicing summer like a cuisinart,
and you feel like a ripe strawberry being dipped
into a warm bath of dark chocolate.

Because it's just too beautiful on this June morning
sitting at a cafe across the bay from Alcatraz
to get trapped in the giant forest of serious questions
about global warming and nuclear winter.

Instead, I'm going to push my oar against the dock and let the moon's
invisible fingers knead the tide back and forth beneath me
careful not to open a can of worms that could rouse
the dormant deep ones that are just waiting to swallow me whole.

FAITH

My brain is a San Francisco apartment—
8 different people congested into a closet
that no single one of them could afford.

It began when I started following you like a lost beagle through
our counterfeit neighborhood, but your indiscernible shape
was always dancing like carbon monoxide fumes behind a bus.

That's when you crawled into my head like an earwig with its
caliper tail, and spray-painted two apocalyptic eyes on the unsuspecting
walls so I'd know that someone's always appraising my thoughts.

I would have taken a shotgun to the ribcage for you,
or at least a severe tongue-lashing from strangers
dropping steamroller insults flattening me as they pass.

I still count minutes like a kindergartner trapped
in rainy day recess board games, while water pools
into oil residue rainbows on broken blacktop

waiting for a ray of sunlight to carve through the deluge
and bend arcs of temporary color the way torches from
a distant mob look like the ocean trembling under the moon.

ABANDONMENT RELIGION

I was born on a flat earth
scared of campfire shadows
and shooting stars,
always said "Amen"
before sinking my fork
into leftover tuna casserole

careful not to cough
up a 4-letter word.
I would never even dip
a toe into the frigid
discipline of my father's
leather belt strap

instead diving under
the bunkbed to hide.
Temptation was drug store
lemonheads trying to sneak
into my empty pockets
but God's toolbox

had fire, famine, and floods.
But fear is like hand-me-down
jeans already worn thin
in the knees, too many
more bedside prayers
and they'd rip wide open.

I'm a failed prophecy
etched on the inside of a cave
that anthropologists
will studiously scribble
down and debate
how to interpret it.

THE GOVERNOR IS PREDICTING A DROUGHT YEAR

Geraniums slouch
in their terra-cotta pots
like remedial students
while out of work weathermen
are scratching their heads
in the unemployment line
wondering why God can't shed
just a few tears.

But he's all dried up.
Nothing left to give
after framing the drywall
of constellations and aiding
touchdown passes.
Space dust and lunar debris
mound like calluses
on the coffee table
and picture frames
he can't stomach
to look at anymore,
just the rumors of grandkids
and distant nephews
who no longer write

or bother to call on Father's Day,
no one around to mop
the fading linoleum floor
or change the burned out stars
in his studio apartment.

HABITS

Moved out as soon as I was old enough to sign a rent check
that wouldn't bounce, couldn't get away fast enough
as if I'd held up the liquor store of adolescence
with a stolen glock riding shotgun in my waistband.

First thing I did for that tiny duplex was pick up
a rusty garage sale lawnmower,
trimmed the dog's tooth grass every Saturday,
and made sure I obliterated the weeds

greening out from the cracks in the driveway
like tiny organic stars against a concrete galaxy
just because they didn't belong there, like a spider
trying to scale the smooth white basin of the bathtub.

Dad religiously did the yard on weekends after bible study.

I suppose it's inevitable to emerge from juvenility,
sprout wings and fly head first into our parents
like an on-coming windshield. Sure, I would never part my hair
down the middle or think a mustache was a good idea.

I'd never buy a station wagon or smother roast beef in horseradish,
but I did start to relish the burnt char of scotch whiskey shoveled
down the furnace of my throat and igniting arguments
from the silence piling up like dry branches,

because it's easier to avoid stepping into the obvious
orange holocaust of a house on fire than it is to notice
the sunrise gradually being poured from a large pitcher
over your silhouette through a mute Winter sky.

QUITTING TIME

I want to decide
when to call it quits.
I checked with God
and he said he'd
turn up his earphones,
look at Jupiter
for a minute, and wouldn't
hold it against me.
I'd like to be really old.
I'd like it to be
a free fall from Half-Dome
plummeting past
the timber line towards
the valley floor meadow
where glaciers and a cacophony
of geologic rumblings
carved granite like an old man
whittling a chunk of pine
on the porch.
Just don't let it happen
in my office, a fluke heart rhythm,
face down on my keyboard
scrolling the letter z down a spreadsheet.
And not on the freeway
where traffic tenses
like new guitar strings
and no one is singing.
And don't let it happen before
the weather turns cool
and I've seen Harbin, China—
the place where my grandfather
fled from his own father,
and 6,500 miles of ocean
couldn't separate the Russian
blood that coursed

through his veins like vodka
through a copper-pot still.
Because I need to see where
it began, the place where
they first found god
in the bottom of a glass.

FILMING THE DOCUMENTARY
OF MY FAMILY

My grandmother always had to put on her face
before leaving the house and don pearl earrings
like glass eyes to go grocery shopping
in the impenetrable fog of the Sunset District

I never think about my great uncle Bill
that died from emphysema and an endless
stream of "shit" and "god damn" pouring
from the river under his breath

I can't interpret the hieroglyphs of my father's
coffee mug stains chiseled into the oak table
or how he could always catch us in a lie
the way a grizzly bear snatches a salmon

My brother and I were distilled from a mash
of Russian winters, San Francisco fog,
and a tablespoon of family repression
fermenting in the bottom of the tank

When the production crew descends
on our house with their artillery of cameras
and rounds of questions, I'll be hanging
the set backdrop waving like a white flag.

ON VISITING MY GRANDFATHER
IN MEMORIAL HOSPITAL E.R.

He's floating on a sea-foam green blanket
with a highway of twisted plastic I.V. tubing
driving moonshine into his veins
like breaching blue whales beneath his skin.
It's the first time I've ever seen
the bare skin of his legs,
the color of a roll of saran wrap
under the hospital lamps.
Blood pressure dipping too low,
I watch the heart monitor as he tells me
about his deceased older brother's
obsession with being a mortician.
How he barely survived
the North African campaign
and was discharged from Sicily
with a gunshot wound to the hand
and ended up in Palm Springs.
How he loved ironing the lapels of jackets
the dead would last be seen in
and the skill of setting cheeks and lips
in just the right expression
as if they were still in a dream,
thinking about flying weightless
across the Atlantic,
the cobalt sky of dawn
rising like a projector screen
above limestone cliffs,
or the thousands of random images
our sleeping brains stitch back together.

GRANDPA WAS A BAKER

There's something almost comforting
in knowing that my grandmother
would iron my grandpa's Munsingwear
boxers until they were as smooth
as the hood of their '56 Olds.
12 hour days elbow deep
in french bread dough just
to make it to Friday night taverns
in the Richmond district. The forearms
of longshoremen and brick layers
lining the bar in their one good suit,

all squirming in starchily-pressed
underwear stiff beneath their trousers.
One gruff line of Pendleton suits
and bowler hats that hid
the calluses and stiff joints
of a generation that erected
skyscrapers and understood,
"You did what you did because
that's the way it was."

Now 84, he asks me about evolution
and why the book of Genesis doesn't
feel the same anymore. His musty
house reeks of old books
and Duke Ellington 45's.
What happens when what you did
doesn't apply anymore? How do you
light the pilot of a digital range,
or drizzle water droplets

into an iron skillet and watch them dance
themselves into steam
and not feel the fragility

of your own skin
that now wears crevices and canyons
carving down vertebrae like time,
the same skin that misses the
firm creases and stitched rigidity
of ironed boxers and books
bound in leather that still made sense.

LETTER TO MY FATHER

I couldn't imagine
bridging the distance
between us,
like trying to picture
the Golden Gate's silhouette
spanning the Bay
before the first girders
were ever sunk.
It was only long rides
in the Datsun wagon
with a broken radio,
roadside weeds
quietly zipping
past my heavy sigh
fogging the window,
and your arm
like a building truss
planted on the wooden
gear shift knob.
I remember you
like this series
of flashcard images:
mustache thick
like a black Russian winter,
a quick dagger of sarcasm
from an unexpected pocket,
and that look none of us
ever talked about but couldn't
shadow away from
like mid-day sun
beating on new asphalt-
you'd be somewhere else if you
could bring yourself to do it.
And I always knew,

like the one kid who saw
the hidden quarter
slipped behind a knuckle.

SILENT KILLER

I held mom's hand until I was eight
because the man with a peppered mustache
and a dented Ford station wagon
was swiping boys from the sidewalks
of Concord. Back then the Zodiac Killer
was still stalking in the gardenias
of Golden Gate Park. Death lurked
on milk cartons, orphaned fliers

stapled to telephone poles, Ouija boards,
chef's knives and unmarked white plastic
bottles breathing beneath the sink.
I would lie beneath Star Wars sheets
afraid that I swallowed a Lego.
But somehow Death's crooked
finger never quite reached the backseat
the way mom's backhand or dad's

frustration could. Never as close
to home as a leather belt
coiled in the dresser's top drawer
or a wooden spoon crouched
at the bottom of a purse.
None as lethal as the suffocating
silence between fathers and sons
that I swallowed like cyanide.

I FREQUENTLY HAVE EXISTENTIAL CRISES ON DAYS LIKE THIS

In the last 24 hours
I extricated lice
from my daughter's
tender scalp,
watched the silent
footage of civilians
being rifled
to the asphalt
in Baghdad,
saw a documentary
on the volcanism
of early earth
with computer
generated graphics
of Pangaea splitting apart
like giant chunks
of construction paper,
and in between mouthfuls
of Reese's Pieces
my son asks me
when the end
of the world comes,
why does it
always explode?

HOW TO SURVIVE
A CROSS-COUNTRY ROAD TRIP

The packed Datsun is loaded like shotgun shells
and we all have itchy trigger fingers.

I yell, "When will it end?" over the precipice of a canyon
but today its echo has laryngitis and called in sick.

Talk radio's muffled AM voice ordering a retreat as I
curl up in the protective armor of the fetal position.

My tongue is a grappling hook I use to scale the silence, my heart
a decommissioned missile silo rusting away in North Dakota.

I carve hash marks into the trunk of the family tree
and trace the interstate map in the veins in my forearm since

they forgot me at the rest stop of the unknown soldier
that smells like the rotting corpse of Christmas decorations in June.

MOM

I heard mom say she got in trouble for wearing
bell bottoms and blasting *Purple Haze*.
Her father used smelling salts to keep her and my uncle
awake during church. She ran away and married a man
who threatened to put his head in the oven
when she left him and met my father.

Her pleats and collars were always starched so stiff
that I couldn't imagine her in jeans back then,
like oral societies that pass on legends and myths,

she could not have been real,
could not have cried and bled,
or closed her fingers in the door
of her black '67 VW and screamed.

She cursed her father's strict hand
long before she evolved her own
with my brother and I.

There are no artifacts from that history,
lost cities to excavate or broken fragments
to adorn locked glass cases.

Faint echoes of stories behind her humming
Roy Orbison hint there used to be more
than the salvation she clings to with bible-black tenacity.
I would like to share a smoke and a cup of coffee
with the woman who's hair, I was told,
grew in rebellious curls.

I NEVER LIKED BOLOGNA

or the London Broil mom scorched
in the electric oven with a broken thermostat.
I hated the clockwork regularity
of Friday night tacos,
shredded cheddar in dull Tupperware
bowls, or corn tortillas
saturated in Mazola. I don't remember
much from Concord, or the apartment
in San Francisco across from the bakery.
But I liked it when she cut my hair
over the kitchen's crisscross linoleum,
avocado bath towel draping my shoulders
while Neil Diamond serenaded us Holly Holy
from the living room.

I turned 36 this year,
scarred two tattoos into my back
and argued with my daughter
about the length of bangs
swooping across her glasses.
It's not that I want to be 13 again,
pimples cratering my forehead
or the complicated geography of braces.
I just miss the wonder sometimes—

      the milky mystery of my first orgasm,
      the dry crackle and pale blue smoke
      of that first cigarette behind the garage,
      imagining the complicated mechanics
      of braziers or if the moon's full face
      ever noticed us praying.

I was 18 the last time mom cut my hair,
her arthritis claiming a knick of hair
behind my ear. I miss the closeness

of her fingers, soft as ripe pear flesh
against my scalp and the textured
orange floor of that old kitchen.
It was the only time I ever talked
to her about girls and she just listened.
Maybe it was the sharp slice of crisp
scissors trimming dirty blonde follicles
or that I never looked her in the eye
when I finally understood she wasn't
going to get better or that we would
never be as close as those afternoons
when I confessed I didn't believe in God
and she pretended not to hear me.

ADDICTION

It's odd to think of the word *cleavage*
as relating to boulders broken off
a cliff's face, all voluptuous and dangerous
like the geology that made you and me

or how I sleep with earplugs
so I can only hear the muffled audio
of my own breathing like old records
I carelessly plunge dirty needles into

I've tried quitting you so many times
but always know exactly where I left off,
mid-sentence under a dog-eared page
where I scribbled graffiti in the margins

my thoroughbred heart has trained
its whole life to only run in circles
like adrenaline racing through muscles
toned to the density of a dying star

I come to you with arms
splayed open like a field
of crosses stretched out
in neat rows as the first words

of a storm slowly roll over
your lower lip shaped like the curve
in a psychiatrist's couch
I want to break down in.

THOUGHTS ON FAITH

I'll never forget
the suit jacket sleeves
that never quite fit,
loafers with a penny
tucked under the tongue,
and trying not to fall asleep
as my head gained weight
by the minute. The cheap
clip-on ties that couldn't
hang straight never fooled anyone
or could convince me
that I shouldn't sneak
the junior miss underwear
catalogue into the bathroom.
I remember the first time
I lied and got away with it,
I imagined God taking note
when no one else noticed
and filing it in his dusty ledger
under the "Things To Do" column
along with finishing the platypus
and teaching ostriches to fly.

3.

POST-GRAMMATICAL STRESS DISORDER

"Without realizing it, the individual composes his life according to the laws of beauty even in times of great distress."
— Milan Kundera

TOURING THE OPEN HOUSE OF MILITARY INVENTIONS

I'm drawn in
by the aroma
of fresh baked
cookies wafting
in from the
stainless steel
kitchen, a tea
kettle screaming
on the stove.
There's technology
of red buttons
on control panels
and the choreography
of two synchronized
keys dancing
in the open
living room
to the dull thud of
steel-toed boots
stomping up and
down a fretless bass.
The long spiral
staircase like
an assembly line
leads down
past bedrooms,
the outdated
furniture covered
like ghosts
in white sheets.
I descend
to find
Gutenberg
in the basement

composing
the machined
precision of
movable type
stamping out
pages of
commandments
to love thy
neighbor.

NOSTALGIA NEVER DREAMS IN COLOR [JUNE 5, 2004]

Every old man has a story:
August afternoons at the cannery
or mowing lawns for a nickel.
The Norman Rockwell type
often sit back in their
creaking wicker rockers
and reminisce about that
charcoal-colored morning
when bullets blanketed the beaches.

But America got Alzheimer's.
He forgot that he used to play dominoes
with the Shah and Batista
on Sunday's after church;
the good old days when
Yankee ingenuity showed
the Reds a thing or two.
But some days are slipping away.
America forgot when
he shook hands with Saddam
and the other September 11,
when Pinochet hijacked Santiago.

He's losing all of it.
He can't remember the other kids
that only got hand-me-downs
and left-overs.
He can't see the ones
that never had a summer job
or the ones that never ran
their blistered hands
through freshly cut grass.

CONSTRUCTING THE WEST

I built the Alamo
in fifth grade-
surveyed the boundaries
on a plywood scrap,
stretched out a lake
of Elmer's glue
and sprinkled sand
like ashes of the dead
over the surface.

Balsa wood walls
braced against plastic
Mexican soldiers,
their elongated muskets
frozen mid-aim.
I fashioned Davy Crockett's
coonskin hat from playdough
and baked it till it hardened
like knuckles curling
into a taut fist.

I didn't realize
the early Texans
had lost or what
the phrase
"Remember the Alamo"
even means, but like
most 10 year-olds
that lived huddled
against the salt-kissed
fog of the Pacific, I just
assumed we always won.

AMERICA MOVES
INTO THE NEIGHBORHOOD

You came for the gold
but stayed for the land,
it wasn't easy work at first
but without a down payment
and a credit check
it was a head start.
Sure, there were already
a few neighbors scattered
about like sparse white clouds
in an April sky, but their tents
were easily moved out of the way.

From dense birch tree forests
you built fences, milled paper,
and drew lines of latitude
and longitude, because
the gentle curves of roaming
bison painted on cave walls
or petroglyphs etched
in sandstone would never
hold up in court against
maps and survey lines
intersecting at right angles.

INAUGURATION

My eardrums take a shellacking every time
you open the gaping sinkhole magnifying
across the fault lines of your geologic face,

and if I dig deep enough I'd discover a core of solid
black malignancy spawning lies like maggots
orbiting the gravity of your desolate world.

THE COLD WAR

Everyone in Leningrad
wore the same cheap
knock-off tennis shoes
and stood in bread lines
while we marched
through Gemco
pissed off that mom
only let us pick out
healthy cereal from
the bottom shelf.

A WALKING DISASTER

My emotional baggage is a broken suitcase
    duct-taped together and lost in another airport.
My credit rating is so low it requires quantum
    mechanics to compute.
My plans all fall through like a chuteless paratrooper
    dropped behind enemy lines.
My fillings need fillings and my blind doctor uses
    a metal detector like a stethoscope to detect my ticking heart.
My regrets are so expensive
    they need financing.
My nightmares smother me like the weight
    of too many *S's* in Mississippi.
My home is a fourth-grade model of a California Mission
    with miniature copies of the unfinished gospels splayed across a table.

UNFINISHED BUSINESS

The spider inside my dashboard quit today,
threw his hardhat at the foreman
and walked off in a huff the way
only someone with eight legs could do.

HALLEY'S COMET

Halley's Comet came hurling by in 1066
when William the Conqueror won the Battle of Hastings.
The pope tried to excommunicate it in 1456
as an agent of the devil.

In 1986 my father drove us out to Gravity Hill,
and while clutching styrofoam cups of 7-11 hot chocolate,
we stared at it, suspended like gunshot residue across the sky.

I don't think we even knew what it was,
but isn't it only ever the things we don't understand
that make us wonder or bring us together?

Like our ancestors lying back on a bed of leaves
inventing the word *stars*, or how we would huddle together
in the dark with closed eyes and open palms
waiting out lightning storms.

I want to open my eyes and wonder at galaxies
and string theory, vibrating like music through our atoms,
and I want to wonder at the world through the Dr. Seuss eyes
of a five-year-old when the world only existed in primary colors.

But I also want to look at the world through the eyes
of an opium-infused beggar on the streets of Calcutta,
and through the eyes of a heart-attack intensive care unit
hospital victim just so that I never take this life for granted

because every day kids are cutting themselves just to feel alive
while we go on piercing each other with the poison of our words
born out of ignorance and fear because we have forgotten
where we came from, and I'm still not quite sure sometimes.

But back in 1789, the philosopher David Hume
thought that comets were the reproductive cells,

the sperm and the egg of planetary systems
and that planets were produced
through some kind of interstellar sex.

While that's probably not true, how beautiful to imagine
galaxies and stars colliding, celestial orgasms
spanning across light years and the embryonic heartbeat
of newly formed pulsars beating out rhythms
louder and larger than our imaginations could ever hold on to.

ECLIPSE

We try to flex our scarecrow arms,
one pointing East and one West
but can't so much as wrinkle
our red flannel shirts like the ghost
reflexes of amputated limbs
our brain stem still tries to twitch.
We've allowed the caked-in dirt
to settle into our overalls
that no longer scare away blackbirds.

This morning I felt sorry for the moon
dissolving into orange over the Oakland hills
because maybe he just wanted to get some sleep.
Too tired from working the night shift
the same way he does every night.
Does he ever cuss under his breath
at 24 hour drive thru's and the AM/PM
around the corner, or tell his boss
to fuck off? Is he jealous that Jupiter
has four of him to share the burden?
Or does he yearn to unravel
his clenched fists, show us
his worn out palms, and swallow
the courage to ask for a raise
he knows he has no chance of getting?
So he buries his head in a pillow
and tries to fall back asleep
until about once a year
when he's finally heard one too many
serenades from clichéd lovers
and every basset hound
in the Western Hemisphere
is barking at him, he storms
upstairs at noon
and blocks out the sun

like a swollen knuckle
swallowing a wedding band.

Frustrated ambition so bright
it scorches the black ants
coursing through the hollow veins
of our straw bodies—
the ones we haven't even begun
to start using.

POST-GRAMMATICAL STRESS DISORDER

Written with Cody Mahler and performed as Comma Sutra

On average, we are being bombarded by 2,500 advertisements,
sales slogans and product brand name logos every single day
and if you strip all of those messages down to their core, they
are telling you that your life is insignificant without them.

That's because the culture of consumerism
has dumbed down intelligence to the lowest
common denominator so that all you really recall
are the catch-phrases that trigger the mindless
consumer impulse in your brain to recall
what's on the 99-cent value meal.

And how do they do it?
By holding words and language hostage:

Imprisoning images inside advertisements
and hollow sales slogans designed to sell
you the same shit with a trendy new name,

well words used to mean something,
back when people refused to burn books
and became martyrs and messiahs,
poets risking their lives to weave the subtle
linguistic tapestry of satire, long before language
was kidnapped by Madison Ave. and words
were sold into slavery and forced to make
the Middle Passage from definition to commodity,

back when the relentless pursuit of perfection
meant more than just an over-priced Lexus
with heated seats and extra-large cup holders,
because it's about time we took language back
and gave words their freedom, releasing them
like orphans from the half-way houses of advertising.

And it's not that I'm trying to complain,
I just don't equate *regular* or *super-size*
with choice, any more than I think lining up
at Starbuck's to drop $5.50 on a
triple-venti-decaf-non-fat-caramel-
vanilla-iced-no-foam-cinnamon-latte
is going to make me sophisticated.

Why do we need to use geckos to sell
car insurance, and Clydesdale horses
and naked women just to sell cold beer
as if an erection was the only
language a man can speak?

Every day, we are raising an army of acronyms,
like wounded soldiers, we're amputating letters
like limbs off of words just to make
them fit into text messages

well WTF because OMG I want to scream
sometimes because I don't want to live
in a world where every word and phrase
has been commodified, re-packaged
and sold back to me, where any two-foot
square tile space above a public urinal
is plastered with a McDonald's ad
telling me that I'm loving it,

because the articulate perfection
of the right combination of words
is like unlocking the hidden nuclear
power of the atom that can start wars,
move entire continents, and can make
the icy walls that we build around
ourselves melt in a second,
because sometimes words
are all we have left to give.

THROWING IN THE TOWEL

The sun
gave up
and called
it quits,
passed out
on the couch
after 4 shots
of whiskey
and a wobbly
stumble back
to his cramped
apartment.
Holes melting
through his
spotted liver
and the
occasional
flare up
that could
end in
closed fists
and open
wounds.
One more
late rent
notice
tacked to
the broken
door frame
and he'll
be out on
the street,
and we
will squint
shadowless

at the
ravenous
black hole
quietly
devouring
the last
fading crumbs
of blue sky.

4.

EAVESDROPPING
ON ANGRY WEATHER

*"The danger of the road is not
in the distance, ten yards is far
enough to break a wheel."*
— *Meng Chiao*

I ALWAYS GET TO THE AIRPORT TOO EARLY

I just know TSA is waiting to snap
five fingers into a blue latex glove
and explore my inner thigh with all
the curiosity a tomb robber would
show the inside of a sarcophagus,

as if there was some secret message
stamped in braille on there telling them
what I carry hidden inside my veins:

like the shame from shooting a horned toad
with a BB gun in second grade
because Tanner called me a pussy,

how the jelly orbs of eyes froze open on top
of that toad's gnarly-spotted head when he plummeted
off the perch of a fence post,

or the gravity generated by us spinning
in circles with arms helicoptering towards
an adolescent sky we couldn't reach,

but here I am at the airport waiting
to sit at 30,000 feet and gut open
a tiny bag of pretzels and pretend to sleep,

because it hurts to look at some people
with these spheres in my head
that cut like sea glass blinking
greyer with each year that passes.

Soon I'll be like the old man next to me
that orders tomato juice
and tries to rub out the arthritis

from his left thigh like wringing
a ripe lime into a Bloody Mary.

Soon I'll be the Montgomery Wards
of the neighborhood, a pile of sand
on the beach where a castle once stood,

God I want to grab the past like a palm tree
spewing its fountain of leaves and shake loose
its logic until equal signs break their parallel world,

where I clench my eyelids
like a last prayer before
the switch is flipped and unleash

a hurricane of wishes barreling
through my breath to smoke out
the candles that are saluting my years,

as if it's some great accomplishment
not to step into oncoming traffic or
not to dive head first into the shallow end.

No, it's not admirable to just keep stealing
oxygen from the world, eat breakfast
and step into the bright blue morning
without a parachute.

FOR SHUTTLE A, TAKE DOOR #1

Perhaps it's the yellow zone, green curb,
multitude of signs, arrows, and automated doors
of O'Hare airport on a rainy June day
that makes me wonder how we ever
managed to crack open a coconut.
How did we ever spark two stones and discover
we could ignite our own piece of the sun,
or that if we rubbed our genitals together
long enough the big bang
could keep happening beneath the sheets?

A taxi cab driver from Somalia
with chiseled features and wire-framed
horn-rimmed glasses tells me,
"Chicago's weather
is like an angry woman."
It's pouring rain and the puffed cheeks
of the wind are inverting umbrellas
showing me their wire skeletons.
I'm walking down Michigan Blvd.
drenched to my bones
and stop in a hotel bar for a Manhattan.
All hotel bars are the same,
and I'd much rather be scrunched
on the torn synthetic vinyl
of a yellow cab listening to him
tell me how he fished from an 8-foot
boat in the Indian Ocean
a year ago while his wife
draped silk nets between two date trees.

I suppose the world is better off
with one less fisherman
and one more taxi-cab driver.
After all, who needs to learn

how to wield two rough pieces of flint
when you have matches.

THE PHILIPPINES

The Eastern Pacific sun
exhales on me like an old drunk.
Sweaty burnt flesh of coconut meat
saturates the heavy layers
of dust and salt sticky air
of General Santos City.

Fire ants navigate scorching
pavement under foot while
3-year-olds cling to the rusty
gas tanks of haggard Honda
cycles under their fathers,
screaming down the highway
past dwarf banana trees
with emerald leaves
like webbed fingers.

Extremes bombard us daily
but like ecstatic new lovers,
we can't see them hovering
like a looming typhoon
idling quietly off shore.

I've seen 3 countries in 4 days.
New wealth, like an impatient
toddler kicking dirt into
his mother's dress
creeps out the cracks
in the sidewalk. A twig-thin
boy the age of my son
scurries to the taxicab
window begging.

All the staff look me
square in the eye,

call me sir
and wait patiently
like dark clouds gathering
behind a Manila sunset.

TEXAS

I'm barely coherent
in an art gallery in Texas,
trying to stumble through
a wedding toast after
too many glasses
of cheap cabernet,
words blurring together
like trying to interpret

hieroglyphs etched
in sandstone.
I drift outside for a smoke
and stand reminded of Modesto,
like the reunion of old friends.
The Winter sun hangs low,
blinding the freezing wood pile
bleeding with rust from old nails.

Time is slow and frost is
beginning to blanket everything.
I expected expansive vistas
and everything to be big here.
Instead, the long drive
through Fort Worth felt like
the CA Central Valley,
like highway 99

through Turlock;
only as exotic as contemplating
bullet holes in the back
of pick-up trucks, or
meticulous metal sculptures
crafted from old engine parts
and one family playing God
in a ranch just outside of Crawford.

GREEN THUMB

This afternoon is oozing
through the faded plank decking
of the Queen Bean Cafe,
and I should be home
pulling weeds from the backyard;
The ones that have taken off their shoes
and made themselves quite comfortable
on the moist mattress of my garden bed.

Wind-blown seeds we can't even see
burrow into our skin and sprout
relatives and acquaintances
we didn't ask for. I only remember
planting lavender, pink camellias,
and azaleas, but spend more time
trying to extract the impacted roots
of random people that have nestled
into my head like wisdom teeth.

Like the woman who's wheezing
from an asthma attack
as she rifles through her tired canvas purse
for a Virginia Slim and an absent match.
Her white knuckles clutching
between aching breasts, she grips her chest
as if it was going to dart in front of a bus
and asks Ed for a light.

I don't understand her orange crocs
or the pink and white plaid capri's
that have seen better days,
or why I even notice her
and the other nomads
that frequent this place.

If only they knew
how much I tend to them,
how familiar the prickly veins
of their rough, jagged leaves
are to my fingers, or

how carefully I release
their dandelion limbs
into the wind.

STANISLAUS COUNTY

I used to be addicted
to the crossword
and syrupy coffee,
the avalanche
of raw sugar boulders
tumbling into a mug
and watching old Jim
dump salt like hail
on poached eggs.

Someone started planting
tract homes over almond tree
roots, while the dust
of old farm stories
still settled into the grease-
grimed tables.
I used to pray back then
before I migrated
to a shoebox in Berkeley,

where no one
does the crossword
and coffee only comes
in a scalding paper cup,
where I can't forget
the 110 degree summers
building tomato pallets
in Ceres and struggling
to sleep where the sidewalks
still blister at midnight.

AUTUMN

Today, I feel like the fifth horseman:
neutral, khaki-colored apathy trailing
behind the other four, like someone
waiting on a laundromat bench,

feeling as mundane as a Tuesday
in a month with no holidays,
so ordinary that I almost completely
forgot how the smell of new rain dripping

like perfume off the bark of redwoods,
or the shapely legs of a wrought iron chair
on the patio confiding in the fallen leaves,
or a sliver of orange moon like a spark

can incite the riot lurking behind my eyes
slowly stirring like constellations,
threatening to step on the land mine buried
just below the shallow surface of my chest.

6 MONTHS AS A TEMP WORKER

Bruce had skin
like a worn out set
of Michelin tires.
He'd sharpen his thumb
and forefinger on the dull-grit
sandpaper of his chin
as I could hear him thinking,
"This kid will never make it."
Tossed me and my torn up
Chuck Taylor's on the drill press
that inhaled me like a great white
shark's gaping unhinged jaws.
I was fresh meat,
130 pounds at best.

They all laughed
when I showed up.
I would have too.

Hostess apple pie
lunchbreaks from
the roach coach
on the creosote stained
railroad ties
of south 7th street,
in the boiler room
of a Central Valley
summer that could melt
anyone's ambitions
down to a rusted stain
on the side of the canal bank.

3 months later
tunneling through
earth's gravelly

surface with a sweat
soaked pick-axe
for the new Kaiser offices,
felt like I was always
transferring dirt and shit
from one heap to another.

It lasted just
long enough
for calluses
to emerge
like punctuation
on nearly
every appendage
of my stickly frame,
long before they started
to grow on the inside,
like vast underground
caverns sculpted
one quiet drop
at a time.

THE ANDES

The high desert
bleeds yellow
pink and red
from its arid soil
dyeing quinoa,
potatoes, and
llama wool
draping the parched
skin of farmers
who wear their
jagged features
like weathered
mountains
of granite.

Each thin breath
drowns under
an ocean
of blue sky,
all the gold
and copper
gouged out
of mountains
that arc
like a broken
spine above
the jungle.

This is forgotten land,
forgotten people,
but they envelop
themselves
in blazing reds
and yellows
that spill across

the rocky earth
once submerged
under some
ancient ocean.

A Quechua woman
with almond skin
smiles, drapes
me in a white
woven scarf
and softly
kisses my cheek
as we float
precariously
above tectonic
forces quietly
plotting their
next maneuver.

PRACTICING SPANISH

1.
I'm the albino
guerilla, the odd
zoo curiosity
everyone lines
up to see.
Their eyes
expanding like
growing stars
when I stand,
clear my throat
and let the
first words
trickle out
of the new
plumbing in
my throat.

2.
The perfect
grammar
of sonic jets
are breaking
the sound
barrier far
above me
while my
broken words
sputter out
like a rusted
VW bus inching
up an overpass.

3.
I leave
a trail of
shrapnel
as I decimate
rolling r's
to rubble
and randomly
stab accent
marks through
innocent
vowels,
because
sometimes
it takes
more than a
mispronounced
"hello" to
break the ice,
sometimes you
need dynamite.

EAVESDROPPING

"I'd like to go to Australia, but not to the outback,"
says the retired couple propped in armless chairs
sitting next to me. But what's to see only on the edges?

The Sydney Opera House about to set sail?
Distant kiwi trees waving across the sea from New Zealand, or
coastline thin as malnourished poetry begging for a metaphor?

Why wouldn't you go far out into the interior
and dive into the ocean of red soil
swirling like Jupiter's giant spot in the center

to feel what it's like to plunge
your arms deep into the rusted sand
oxidizing around the roots of your fingers

the way a heart surgeon reaches deep into
the cavity of an open ribcage to cradle the lust
of silent ambitions desperate to scream out.

THE EXCHANGE RATE
OF A PILGRIMAGE

A girl preserved
under grey plaster
sleeps in a glass coffin
inside a cathedral
in Guadalajara.
Polaroids of her family
circle above her
like cherubs
around a fountain.
Worn rosaries
turn like rusted
bicycle chains
around the wrists
of grandmothers,
and I wish that
I felt blood oozing
from the palms
of my hands
or heard the screams
of trumpets
kicking down
ancient stone walls
as I look at her,
but I don't.
I drop 5 pesos
into the empty
vessel of
a beggar's
cupped hands,
his face—
the black box
of a missing
plane no one
is looking for.

5.

SMOOTH CURSIVE &
RAW OYSTERS

*"I feel as if heaven lay close upon
the earth and I between them both,
breathing through the eye of a needle."*
— Lawrence Durrell

MODERN ART

I was assembled from
3 different jigsaw puzzles,
the pieces that didn't fit
hammered into place

   my head a swirling chunk of Starry Night
   my torso, Washington crossing the Delaware
   an arc of Saturn's rings where my feet should be

the curator has found
a suitable corner to hang me,
right next to a silhouette
on a chunk of sidewalk

dug up from Hiroshima,
the experimental art of atoms
dropped on a concrete canvas
unframed, unsigned.

SILENT FILMS

Tip-toeing on the ledge
of precarious lips
like a tightrope walker
in the 1920's spanning
Niagara Falls, or thumbing
his suspenders under the charcoal
rim of a bowler hat
on the thirtieth story
of a steel-framed skyscraper.

I never understood
why early comedy revolved
around balancing wooden chairs
on iron girders and the hairpin turns
of Model T's weaving
like sunlight through streetcars.
Maybe it's because they're
immortal- some bizarre, indestructible
race of keystone cops and racketeers
who could plummet like sacks
of powdered concrete from bridges
and shake off the dust
like nothing happened.
You didn't need to be able
to read lips to interpret
their unworldly cue-card
dialogue and furled brows
that couldn't die no matter
how many times the mob
filled 'em full of lead.
They just kept breathing.

I bet they wish they couldn't
take a bullet now-
still running around

the back alleys
of Hollywood sets behind piles
of orange extension cords
coiled like pythons
and defeated spot lights
with their heads slouching down set.
They lived through Hoover Blankets
and the Depression because tommy guns
and barrel rolls over cliffs
never did the job.
But nowadays it takes flesh
and dirty fingernails to take a bullet,
to get choked up over death,
or wrap fingers around a rubber cord
ready to pull the plug,
because life was not always
meant to be continued.
Some scenes need to close
the third act with a drawn
burgundy curtain telling
the audience in no uncertain
terms it's time to go home.

THE OPERATION

I asked
the doctor
to replace
all my
broken organs
with new
appliances—
no more
complicated
biology or
chemistry
to diagnose,
just an
alternating
current
flowing like
drunk confessions
through my
copper veins
to the blinking
cursor in
my eyes
waiting
for someone
to press
the enter key.

MANNEQUIN MAKER

I envision him alone
in a cavernous shop
surrounded by hundreds
of rubber chin and cheek
molds, rusted tool chests
full of synthetic eyelashes
black as scorched engine oil,
and wigs racked on wall hooks
like wooly carcasses.

I picture him shaping
her vacuous lips to the fullness
of ripe tomatoes, assembling
spindly hands onto bolted
forearms outstretched
like empty oak branches.

I can see him
selecting a pair of legs
from a holocaust pile
of plastic body parts
and fashioning feet
into stiff arches.

I imagine it's a solitary task
constructing a human body-
so elegant, so fragile
and awkward,
a skill no one
has yet perfected.

THE MECHANIC

My heart is
due for its
100,000 mile
tune-up,
maybe a new
valve job.
I prop open
the hood
of my ribcage,
unscrew
each ventricle
and scrub
the lustful
residue off,
promising
myself that
this time
I will only
fill it with
high-octane
emotions,
the kind
I can
never
afford.

BELIEF

I always used to imagine God just sitting there
admiring his handiwork from an old creaking oak chair,
ceaselessly pointing and directing angels, seraphs,
and cherubs running around invisibly engineering
tiny corrections of freeways near misses, would-be flat tires
that just made it home and tilting my head
3 degrees to the left to avoid a head-on
collision with the shower head.

But I could never comprehend the ones
that didn't make it: like the tree limb
that landed on my cousin, the freak meteorite
that scratched open the sky to crash
on a woman's leg in Toledo, why my grandfather
couldn't beat cancer long enough
to see me take my first steps or why

my mother has swallowed a medicine cabinet
every morning, self-injections of insulin
and nitroglycerin just to keep her velvet throat
from closing and suffocating herself
in the queen-sized bed that she has lived in
for the past 20 years trying to whitewash history
with nothing more than a powder-blue handicapped
placard swaying from the rear-view mirror

and the cracked spine of her leather-bound bible
coughing up old-testament plagues and prophecies
that cannot exorcise the paralytic demons of arthritis
possessing her hands that never stop shaking,

because she can't stop believing. And I don't blame her
for squinting into the sky looking for those eternal arms
to point in her direction the same way I used to. But what
I can't figure out is why we started looking towards heaven

in the first place instead of looking into each other.
Why did we ever start looking for divinity in shrouds
and petroglyphs, books and rituals?

But despite it all,
I can still see God's exhales
fogging up the windows
of my mother's eyes
trying to shine through.

And I don't need ministers or monks to see the divinity
in the faces of my children who are dreaming
of a bigger world to play in, because we have made
it so small by constructing fences out of crucifixes
and 30-foot high walls growing like olive tree branches
through occupied territories in Palestine

when we should be writing poetry
instead of prayers, sacrificing metaphors
instead of martyrs, because we can
make this world so beautiful
if we would stop waiting for
someone else to do it for us.

ALL HE EVER WANTED WAS EVERYTHING
(For Joshua)

Only solitary men have visions,
like the one who navigates annotated sidewalks
in a wool cardigan,
green like Spanish olives.

Plagued with philosophy and a haiku smile,
he drops a nod
and raises an eyebrow
to the urban prophets
perched on the concrete pulpit
of a traffic island.

On his way downtown,
the streets are littered
with five o'clock shadows
and a November fog so thick
that even history has to stop
for a cup of coffee;
but he can't be slowed down today.

His visions burn
his pregnant heart,
the way Moses
saw his own biography
in the silhouette of Yahweh
while he was warming
his hands next to a burning bush.

Something calls him too.
Perhaps it isn't an angel
telling him to recite,
and maybe it's not God,
the voice of reason,
or the grandeur of prophethood.

But he looks for it
in the first moments after revelation
when he rubs his tired eyes
and carries his daughter to bed.

Sometimes his visions need room to breathe,
so he slips outside,
lights his soot-stained pipe
and parts the waters of a storm
descending like an Egyptian cavalry
on the streets of Santa Cruz.

CONFESSIONS OF AN 18-YEAR VEGETARIAN

Bacon is a gateway drug.
It started innocently enough-
two strips, applewood cured,
panting on a paper towel
fresh from an iron skillet.
Within a week
I was on to pepperoni
and pork tamales,
rolling masa on Christmas
and tasting pork pozole.
I swore I'd never slip
into hamburger,
but then In & Out
whispered my name
from an alley corner.
Within two weeks I sunk
my virgin steak knives
into boneless rib eyes
heavy with marbled
lines of fat.
If I start smuggling
peppered jerky
in the soles of my shoes
through the security gate
don't be alarmed,
it's for personal use
and not to be peddled
on schoolyards.

THE AUTOBIOGRAPHICAL DIRECTOR IN MY HEAD

The narrator recites
each day's episode
into the microphone.
Every orchestrated
word caught
on celluloid,
wrapped like
mummified tape
around reels
and buried away.
I'm addicted to
watching reruns of
*"Abandoned at
the Auto Show
When I was 7"*
and *"Renovating
Closet Alcoholics"*
but when the
lights are out
I can't stop
suffering
self-inflicted
wounds from
re-watching
the pilot of
*"Blunt Force
Trauma: love's
first blow
to the head"*
over and over,
the lacerations
cutting deeper
with each
successive frame.

SUNDAY AFTERNOON
AT CAFFE TRIESTE, SF

I thought about coming here all day
because this is where literary giants
once roamed and corralled their untamed
ambitions under portraits of Pavaroti,
Burt Lancaster and Tony Bennett.
The slippery sex of their words
slithered down throats like raw oysters,
and everyone knew *Howl* by heart.

But today, the tweed-clad mustache
at the corner table, who has his facts
all wrong, dribbles into the ear of a dusty-haired
woman who probably once loved him
about what's wrong with college
these days and how he got a BA
for two hundred dollars in the Sixties.

I'm ten feet away holding up the aging ass
of the line like threadbare bell-bottoms
and can still hear him mumbling
pseudo-philosophical jargon occasionally
peppered with the word *naked*
loudly tossed in. There's one empty island
of a chair in a sea of lap-tops
and I pull out a tablet
of college-ruled and a blue Papermate.

This city weaned beat poets and Black Panthers
on the foggy arteries of its hilly landscape. God
created man on the sixth day and today I'm writing
my ninety-fourth poem on the fading formica
table tops that have slept here for decades.
I imagine them releasing pleasant sighs
and soft murmurs as they relax

under the gentle massage of my ball-point
pen through the paper.

The tense "ooh" they cringe as I dot an *i*
and the throaty "mmm" they drool out
as I curve a slow *s*. Thankful that I write
in a smooth cursive, they wink me
a silent "thank you" as I throw
my messenger bag over my shoulder
and slip out the door; grateful they
didn't have to sit through another tattoo
session of studious fingers needling a keyboard.

WHY I WRITE AT COFFEE SHOPS

Because I get nowhere
writing in my living room.
Like trying to run in dreams,
my rubbery insect legs sludging
through dripping tree sap.
It's the possibility of seeing something
that wasn't meant to be poetic:
a lit cigarette flicked
across the sidewalk sparking
off a navy blue fender,
shadows evolving across a white wall,
or the city exhaling through a man-hole
cover on J Street. As if I'm
waiting to see the one perfect image
that will lead me towards the last line
of a poem that's just out of reach:
like a child jumping in slow motion
to catch a yellow balloon
rising in the September wind.

TRYING TO WRITE
AT CAFE MILANO

I'm choking
on verbs
like a hunk
of undercooked
steak stuck
in my throat.
Rachmaninov
in one ear
and homeless
John in the other
like two prize
fighters that will go
the full 12 rounds.
The cement grey
sky is flattening
the city to rubble
as the last
discernible notes
of 'Round Midnight
are strangled out
of a saxophone.

TIME IS ALL TOO RELATIVE

4 dreams could live entire lifetimes
in the split-second between the headlight flash
of lightening and the celery stalk snap of thunder,
but waiting in a maze of morning traffic tail lights
feels like a 12-part documentary series
on the anatomic intricacies of a fern's spore sac.

Or my grandfather trying to open the deadbolt
of his security screen door- the long retractable chain
of his belt-hook ring zipping out of its chamber
high school janitors would be jealous of,
and his 83 year old ears that can't hear me thinking,
"Hurry up!"

Or the inevitable single mother of seven
in the express line doubting the 98 cents of a Zagnut bar
or the pound of fuji apples she swears only weigh 14 ounces.

But somehow I can count on the fleeting minutes
of our interlaced fingers sprinting by like Kenyan marathon runners
with the wind pressing into their backs.
There never seems to be enough time to dissolve
into each other beneath lazy ceiling fan afternoons,
and the conspiracy of the hour hand thrusting itself
right past 4 and 5 pulling its shadow on top of 6.

Apparently he forgot about all the time I saved
taking back roads and skipping lunch.
Peripheral images of you like ghosts
dance by through the staggered choreography of a flipbook
and I wonder how long I can roll a grape
around my thirsty tongue before I take a bite.

WE DON'T KNOW
HOW GRAVITY WORKS

You've never
known how
to breathe
in melody,
only staccato
rhythms like
blinking
tail lights
over a cliff,
heavy as
a 40-story
crane exhaling
steel girders.
Your eyes are
an avalanche of
unstable earth
that sound like
the first night
our bodies
went into
orbit around
each other,
racing like
electricity
around a
copper-coiled
generator
the closer
we came.

LOVE

My own devices
are unwieldy
analog machines
from another
decade that
I shouldn't be
left alone with,
pulling apart
the frayed reels
of nostalgia
under the
dripping amber
of the closet
light bulb
looking for
the still frame
of the day
you unloosed
the mooring
ropes of our
agnostic
love like a
sailboat full
tilt in a storm,
the keel cutting
like a plow
through acres
of fertile ocean.

ETCHED IN STONE

We all had that one friend that we
carried around in our backpacks
just because deep down he made us
feel a little better about ourselves,

the one who couldn't scale the gym rope
or start the cold engine of his lips to talk to girls.
He tried to ignite the same anecdote about
Rilke and Rodin that we'd heard a dozen times
that never sparked a primordial conversation into life.

He's the one you haven't thought about
since he got you that summer job
steam-cleaning carpets at Ross
and wiping down Smitty's Bar
at 6am after the comatose regrets

of someone's last paycheck
smoldered away in an ashtray
between half-empty mugs of distraction.

Ultimately, he'll end up as a footnote
clinging to the bottom of a page
in a thrift store set of encyclopedias-
the kind destined to be picked up

by a man, newly single in his fifties
trying to fill the empty bookshelves
that once cradled portraits of arms
holding each other so assuredly

that you'd swear nothing could
tear apart the fabric of their space,
their restless eyes trembling
like newly discovered stars.

AN IMAGINARY LEGACY

I want to be a stowaway
on your train of thought,
with my red bandana bundle
bobbing over my shoulder
like a ripe apple in September.
I dangle one leg out
of the open boxcar
and hope we're heading
towards a daydream

where you'll do nothing
more than eat cherries
on a large balcony
and pluck the stems
from your fresh lips,
and I'll be a head of state
behind a mountain
of decrees awaiting
the precision of my signature

and processions of black
sedans marching like ants.
They'll pile tulips and lilies
beside my river of speeches,
and I will fall like loose change
from the pockets of
children along the tracks,
my copper minted face
flattened on the rails.

ACKNOWLEDGEMENTS

Grateful acknowledgment is made to the following publications in which some of these poems, sometimes in earlier versions, originally appeared:

"The Governor is Predicting a Drought Year" previously published in *Penumbra*, 2009; "Mannequin Maker" previously published in *Collision*, 2010; "Silent Films" previously published in *Collision*, 2008; "Quitting Time" previously published in *Song of the San Joaquin*, Winter 2010; "For Shuttle A, Take Door #1" previously published in *Penumbra*, 2010; "Texas" previously published in *Song of the San Joaquin*, Winter 2010 & *Collision*, *2010* and nominated for the Pushcart Prize in 2009; "Grandpa Was a Baker" previously published in *Penumbra*, 2010; "Pez" previously published in *Collision*, 2009; "Why I Write at Coffee Shops" previously published in *Collision*, 2010 & *More Than Soil, More Than Sky: The Modesto Poets*, 2011; "Sunday Afternoon at Caffe Trieste" previously published in *Penumbra*, 2009 & *Collision*, 2008; "Green Thumb" previously published in *More Than Soil, More Than Sky: The Modesto Poets*, 2011; "Confessions of an 18-Year Vegetarian" previously published in *Song of the San Joaquin*, Summer 2010; "Silent Killer" previously published in *Quercus Review*, 2010 & *More Than Soil, More Than Sky: The Modesto Poets*, 2011; "I Frequently Have Existential Crises on Days Like This" previously published in *Snail Mail Review*, 2011; "Maternal Instincts" previously published in *Naked Knuckle*, 2004; "Stanislaus County" previously published in *Quercus Review*, 2005 & *More Than Soil, More Than Sky: The Modesto Poets*, 2011; "Nostalgia Never Dreams in Color" previously published in *Quercus Review*, 2005 & *Collision*, *2010;* "I Never Liked Bologna" previously published in *Quercus Review,* 2009 & *More Than Soil, More Than Sky: The Modesto Poets,* 2011; "Eclipse" previously published in *Penumbra,* 2008.

I would also like to gratefully acknowledge the help and support of Sam Pierstorff, Stella Beratlis, and Gillian Wegener in helping me to compile and edit this manuscript. I would also like to thank my brother Evan, Joshua Pollock, and Cody Mahler for their continued inspiration and support over the years. I am eternally grateful to the professors and instructors who took me in and nurtured me as I exited one world and entered a larger new one.

ABOUT THE AUTHOR

Chad Sokolovsky is a Bay Area native and graduate of the University of California at Berkeley. His poetry has appeared in *Song of the San Joaquin, Penumbra, Quercus Review, More Than Soil, More Than Sky: The Modesto Poets,* among others and was nominated for a Pushcart Prize. He currently works as a commodity food buyer and serves as an advisor for the CA department of Agriculture's Organic Product Advisory Committee. He lives in Berkeley, CA.

.

www.ingramcontent.com/pod-product-compliance
Lightning Source LLC
Chambersburg PA
CBHW051837040426
42447CB00006B/581